Piano Play-Along

COLDPLAY

Front Cover Image © Victoria Smith / Retna Ltd.

ISBN 978-1-4584-9436-8

HAL•LEONARD®
CORPORATION
7777 W. BLUEMOUND RD. P.O. BOX 13819 MILWAUKEE, WI 53213

Visit Hal Leonard Online at
www.halleonard.com

CLOCKS

Words and Music by GUY BERRYMAN,
JON BUCKLAND, WILL CHAMPION
and CHRIS MARTIN

Lights go out and I can't be saved. __ Tides that I tried to
Con - fu - sion __ nev - er stops. __ Clos - ing __ walls and

swim a - gainst __ brought me down up - on my knees. __
tick - ing clocks __ gon - na come back and take you home. __ I

And noth - ing else com - pares.

EVERY TEARDROP IS A WATERFALL

Words and Music by GUY BERRYMAN,
JON BUCKLAND, WILL CHAMPION,
CHRIS MARTIN, PETER ALLEN,
ADRIENNE ANDERSON and BRIAN ENO

PARADISE

Words and Music by GUY BERRYMAN,
JON BUCKLAND, WILL CHAMPION,
CHRIS MARTIN and BRIAN ENO

FIX YOU

Words and Music by GUY BERRYMAN,
JON BUCKLAND, WILL CHAMPION
and CHRIS MARTIN

THE SCIENTIST

Words and Music by GUY BERRYMAN,
JON BUCKLAND, WILL CHAMPION
and CHRIS MARTIN

SPEED OF SOUND

Words and Music by GUY BERRYMAN,
JON BUCKLAND, WILL CHAMPION
and CHRIS MARTIN

see it then you'll un - der - stand. _____

All those signs, _____ I knew what they

YELLOW

Words and Music by GUY BERRYMAN,
JON BUCKLAND, WILL CHAMPION
and CHRIS MARTIN

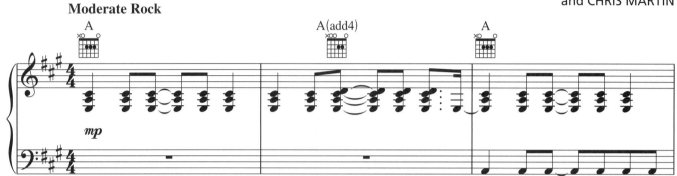

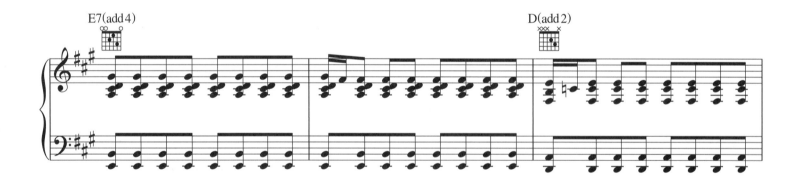

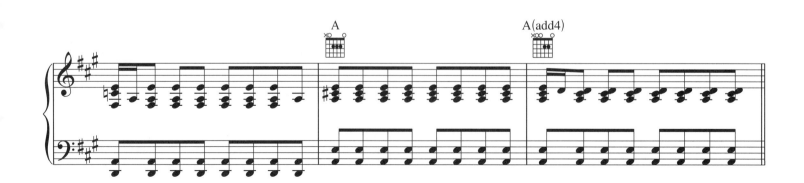

VIVA LA VIDA

Words and Music by GUY BERRYMAN,
JON BUCKLAND, WILL CHAMPION
and CHRIS MARTIN